TEEN EMPOWERMENT THROUGH SOCIAL GRACES

A Guide to Promoting Confidence, Kindness, and Respect

Dr. Hattie Isen

Tinsel Town Publishing

Copyright © 2021 Hattie Isen

All rights reserved

ISBN-13: 978-0-9798592-4-3

No part of this book may be reproduced, or stored in a retrieval system, or transmitted in any form or by any means, electronic, mechanical, photocopying, recording, or otherwise, without express written permission of the publisher.

Cover design by Chris Strain Design
(www.chrisstraindesign.com)

Photos by JustInvision Photography
(iamjustinvision@gmail.com)

Published by Tinsel Town Publishing
(www.tinseltownpublishing.com)

Printed in the United States of America

*A SPECIAL THANK YOU
TO ALL FOR READING.*

*Please visit my website for more information.
www.tipsofthespear.com*

Welcome young friends!

AUTHOR'S NOTE

I have long been an advocate for education and improving educational standards and embracing diverse learners by teaching to the social and cultural context of the classroom. I honestly feel that funding schools in inner-city neighborhoods must be made a priority. Student achievement depends on many things. Today's students are tomorrow's leaders. I hope that this book will help groom young people to meet the challenges they will face with confidence, kindness, respect for others, and respect for themselves.

A positive attitude regarding education must be delivered to today's youth. They must be excited about learning and excited about being a success in life. Academics can be fun, and a learning environment can be fun too. My goal is to help create an educational system that works for all students despite their race and faith. I believe young people feel unprepared for the 'real world' and are concerned about their lack of preparedness in facing what comes after school. This is a valid fear. I hope that my pages instill kindness and comfort, and confidence in all young people who read them.

This book is a learning path. May all who read it get the career they desire and the success they deserve.

Hattie

INTRODUCTION

My mother would often say, "when you go out, whether school or church, remember, charity begins at home. Be kind to others and show your home teachings in what you do and say." When I look back at this today, I cannot help but admire my mother's beautiful practicum. Mom tended to remind her children of the "golden rule," *do unto others as you would want them to do unto you.*

I think my mommy and daddy's personality and character made me the person I am today. Extraordinary in so many ways, I was inspired even by their throwaway moments, the moments that were so casual you hardly knew they were remarkable, but they were. Funny, when I think about it, the value they carried with them as human beings. Fully rounded people, my parents were souls that did not fall. They stood up for who they were and what they believed – within the limitations of civil rights. Their manners were never artificial. They distinguished facts and opinions.

I remember the time when my parents wanted to add another room to our home. The children were excited about it and shared their views, but daddy discussed the reality of paying for it. After sharing the cost of the building and daddy's income, the construction was delayed. Mom shared the skills of her uncle, who was a carpenter. Later, our uncle built the additional room for a very reasonable price.

I learned from this situation how to evaluate conditions. I realized that you have to think problems through to make the right decisions and be a practical and effective decision-maker. I also learned never to give up and never throw in the towel. Just because you can't do something right then, it does not mean you can't do it at all. And it may be frustrating for some, but I don't think complicated situations in life have to ruin your life. You change what you can, identify what you can't change, and develop coping skills to deal with your emotions. I learned you have to be patient.

Patience is not easy, especially when you are young and impatient. But remember, my dear young people, nobody said life is fair. So, I learned from my parents when they got my uncle to build the addition to brainstorm. It would help if you brainstormed potential ways to handle situations. You're likely to have more options than you might think you do and completely surprise yourself.

Spend time thinking about how you can respond to a challenging situation. Even if you can't fix it, you can develop a plan to cope with it. It would be best if you learned how to keep yourself going. It wasn't easy, but I learned how to keep myself going. I learned to identify what is within my control and resolve to make changes for betterment.

I also learned from my upbringing that I should not be afraid to reach out for help if I need it. Challenging situations aren't easy to handle. Asking for help can be a sign of strength and courage and show that you are a real trooper. It shows that you cannot handle whatever it is on your own and that you recognize it. Recognizing your abilities is part of maturity. So, young people, do not be afraid to look for help in various ways to help cope with the challenges you face.

I have tried to live by this standard of excellence and have passed it on to my family. Kindness, respect, and love are what I stand for in life. Breaking down barriers is not a choice and must be a practice. If there is no kindness, there can be no love. If you don't have respect, you cannot have anything. My parents' standard of excellence gives me renewed energy every day to positively impact everything I do in life through the *loving-kindness* of compassion and the beauty of empathic joy.

Happiness in life is a fortune to relish. Life revolves around fun and useful things. But how do we get to joy? By inspiring others with your vision and advocacy for a better, more just world is the answer in my book. Young people be an iconic symbol of peace and truth, and justice for all. There are many doors to be opened in life, so you must live life to the fullest. Be ruled by your passions and advocate for them.

It is essential, young people, that you become survivors in this thing called life. You are a living example of survival. When the chips are down, you rise. You don't let anything keep you down. Grow up with patience and lots of love in your heart. Admire those who are worthy of your admiration. Encourage your friends and family with inspiration and virtue. Let yourself rise to new heights every day.

The ups and downs in life are many. The celebrations can make us happier and set us up for future success. Share your thoughts with family and friends. Talk about your goals. Mentor others. Question unfairness in life. Be productive and be pro-active. Don't allow things to stop you in life. I have not let anything in life stop me. I have not allowed age to stop me! I am a woman, almost eighty, and taking care of a sick sister with cancer.

I take her to doctor appointments, cancer treatments, shop for groceries, and look, I have made time to come out with two books – one is Tips of the Spear – The Hattie Isen Story, which I hope you will read, and the other one is the book you are reading right now. You cannot allow life to sidetrack you. Let your ambitions lead the way to your successes, and remember, not only can your dreams come true, they will come true. I am living proof of survival when the chips are down. I survived and I thrived! I live by two vital principles: love one another (John15:12) and serving as an active deed of love. I am sure you have similar ethics and morals. Remember, the act of serving will not be forgotten by those whom we serve. It moves the hearts of others and offers comfort. I hope my sister feels the results of my service and is blessed.

Can we be happy in a racist world? It is an excellent question, and I ask myself this question a lot. There is surprising joy in life even though the mysterious and unresolved question of why racism exists is yet to be answered, much less resolved. I fear the riddle of racism and its generations of unfair doctrine will live for years to come. Inherit in so many people; we look at a sad world that still feels vindicated for reasons we will never understand. In the telling and retelling of slavery, we can only look at America's history of slavery as a very dark time not only in this country but for the world.

Black people and people of color are loving people who never deserved, endorsed, or accepted slavery. We never enjoyed picking cotton and living in shacks. We never enjoyed separatism or the likes of today's murders and shootings and being the by-products of police brutality. I ask myself if the unfairness will ever stop, but I don't get an answer. Keep asking the question, my young friends. You see, as long as you can still ask the question, there will be an answer. When we stop asking the question, we demonstrate to the world and ourselves that we have given up.

I began this paragraph, making it clear that people of color never deserved, endorsed, or accepted slavery. I can say that some White people did not endorse or accept slavery as well, although only a few during the earlier generations. Some White friends and colleagues have voiced their opinions about racist policies, unequal education, and practices in recent decades. About twenty years ago, I recalled a friend, Vicki Kinder, who spoke out and questioned the leadership of a private school our son was attending for not honoring Dr. Martin L. King's Holiday. Her voice was heard, and changes were made. I will never forget Vicki's concern and advocacy.

Apathy does not live within you. I should hope it does not. Apathetic souls do not rise. They wither and die and do not make a mark on this world. Apathy destroys human beings. Indifference shows that a modern society can become numbed to the fate of its minorities. Did you know that, my young friends? There are more ways of destroying people than sending troops into the streets, storming the radio and television stations, and arresting them. It is when apathy creeps into a person and takes away their hope.

Apathy is a lack of interest, enthusiasm, or concern for anybody and life in general. It also is a lack of interest in yourself. You don't care. You are not motivated, and you have abandoned love and hope. All thoughts of betterment are discarded. It is merely a state of not caring. My young friends, I do believe this is the biggest threat to the Black race. You are our future, and if you don't care and are indifferent, nothing happens. I don't want you ever to feel a lack of purpose, worth, or **meaning** in your life.

My young friends, we don't know if we will ever get back this way again. You may never eat another apple, go to a dance, or buy a gift for someone special after this life. We don't know what happens. Be the most that you can be in this life, my young friends. Life goes by fast. Goodness! I cannot believe I am almost eighty!

I ask you, young people, to think every day about making this world a better place. A significant economic crisis can plunge this country and the world into a deep depression. Do you have ideas so that this does not happen? Do you have pictures, so the banks don't crash, companies don't fold, and do you know how millions of people can stop losing their jobs? What are your ideas? How can you make a better future for all of us? How will you bring ethics and values back to people? How will you make people happy and give them the will to live? What are the coping mechanisms that you suggest? What are your educational and emotional connections to the issues at hand to make the right calls?

What is your plan for establishing international cooperation with other nations? We are one nation and one world. You cannot just act like other countries do not exist. What is your method of diplomacy? Do you believe in the olive branch? The olive is an ancient symbol meaning "let us make peace" and the willingness to bring the conflict to a conclusion. If you extend an olive branch, it means that you want to make peace with someone after an argument, fight, or disagreement. How can we bring this back to current day society? Do you have a plan?

My young friends let's talk about forgiveness. We are a community of remarkable people. But is forgiveness part of our belief and practice? Some of you are shaking your head "No", and some are nodding "Yes." Let me tell you something, my young friends, when you have been hurt or injured by someone or a group of somebody's, you must be the better person and rise. You can shake hands, offer a hug, or maybe a kiss on the cheek and work through it, and forgive. We must forgive to move forward. A white tulip symbolizes forgiveness; if you have trouble telling someone you are sorry and wish for forgiveness and a new beginning, give them these flowers, and start anew. But what does this mean?

It means, my dear friends, that there must be a new way of thinking. The concept of forgiveness constitutes one of the essential fundamentals of the human relationship with God and each other. We must strive to conduct our own lives in the same manner toward others. Since every human being is imperfect and needs forgiveness, we must grow and extend an olive branch, but we must introduce fair thinking.

When people in a relationship or friendship or a family can forgive one another for their flaws and offenses, this process draws them even closer than they would have been had the offense never taken place. But a person or all people involved must commit to change. All people must commit to betterment. If we all are not engaged, then no one is executed, and then nothing can work. Everyone involved must include rigorous self-examination of their behavior and their persona. They must ask themselves how they can be a better person. They must express regret and sorrow and make every effort possible to right the wrong committed. This is how we break down barriers. This is how we create betterment not only for you and me but for the world.

Granting earned forgiveness is an act of social grace that

may be emotionally refreshing, uplifting, and inspiring, and is a distinguishing element of goodness and ethics. It shows proper respect not only for yourself but for how you view others. Embrace remorse with a superhuman determination to make amends with all. Remember, it is for you to know that you forgive.

I don't know why there has to be ugly in the world. I think it's that people don't see each other as human beings. They see one another as better or worse. The distinction has been going on for far too long. Don't tell them, my young friends, show them. Show them you are educated, honorable, and respectful. Show your social graces to the world. Let your kindness to all living things flood the world with goodness.

Young People, you hold the future! You have the key to change. I dream that your hands will hold the hands of future generations. I dream that you will fill the world with confidence, respect, kindness, objective thinking, peace, and love. I pray that your generations will escape the horrors of prejudice and that you can be all that you can be and be human.

I passionately believe that we owe you, young people, a good life. We must protect your futures – leaving it better than we found it. I suggest that all adults advocate for giving young people the love they deserve through guidance, education, and support. When I was young, my knowledge was limited due to racial separatism, but it did not change my dreams, stop my creativity, or stop my imagination. As Albert Einstein quoted, "Imagination is everything. It is the preview of life's coming attractions." Your coming attractions are not far away. I begin this advocacy today, holding hands with every one of you. May this guide of Teen Empowerment be your preparation tool for a secure, respectful, and compassionate future, and also may this piece of literature be a good and valuable friend.

With all my heart and soul, my young friends, I believe you are the change I have been praying for with all my heart.

Hattie

*A good friend
Is life's gem
And makes life
BEAUTIFUL.*

Hattie

Teen Empowerment Through Social Graces

My Dear Young Friends,

How are you? I want to introduce myself to you a bit more. I grew up to become a successful woman and never went down the path of addictions, disrespect, and bad behavior. I have never been self-centered or selfish. I believe in others. I believe in being a great friend and treating others with kindness and respect. It is essential to make and retain friends throughout your life. Trust me on this.

It is also essential to develop a habit of concern for others at the expense of yourself. It is beautiful to be a caring person that is concerned about the problems of others. I have always made my family and friends the center of all my efforts and thoughts. In this way, we acquire confidence and respect and offer goodness to others. When we are respectful and confident, we love ourselves, love others, practice kindness, and break down barriers of hatred.

What is hatred, exactly? Hatred has painted the darkest, most puzzling, and troublesome chapters in the history of all time. The oldest hatred is hostility, bigotry, and prejudice—attitudes like this date back to ancient times. Hatred is based on the other's perception. It has a strong relationship with ourselves, our personal history, and its effects on our personality, feelings, ideas, beliefs, and identity. Jealousy, guilt, and failure can trigger and intensify hatred.

Hatred saddens me. The history of this country is darkened with it. American history is rife with prejudice against groups and individuals because of their race, religion, disability, sexual orientation, or other characteristics. As a country, we've made a lot of progress, but stereotyping and unequal treatment persist. Hatred can make you lose hope and feel despair. If it is directed against you, it is hard to take. We have to feel bad for those who hate.

When an individual or a group encounters significant setbacks, they turn to hate to try effectively or instead more effectively to build their coalitions, get their point across and attract supporters. Groups and online communities use the hate momentum with a terroristic focus—those who commit themselves to more openly violent messages and strategies in service of their racist worldviews. Strings of racially motivated people energize hate movements.

We need to deliver lessons in tolerance and understanding. In this way, we are known for our wisdom and insight. We are known for being filled with love and forgiveness. We are known for our humanness and not for our hatred. We don't always comprehend the meaning of things as they happen because they can trigger events from an earlier point in our lives. I hope, my young friends, that all races and backgrounds can unite and lead the way to destroy hatred, whose ugly head has risen to prominent positions of power in the world today.

Life, at times, can fill you with anxiety and be very stressful. Addictions are not coping mechanisms. Remember, nobody is perfect in life. All you are expected to be in life is the right person, kind to others, and be kind and loving to family, friends, and animals. When I say a good person, I mean a respectful person. Respect the elderly, the sick, and the unfortunate. Admit your mistakes graciously. Keep your momentum going with everything you deal with daily and keep trying to make something good happen in your life and the life of others.

I want to say something else. The White population

needs to understand the Black plight and The Black fight. Whites need to dig beyond mere facts, and look outside the box, and need to understand the Black experience, which includes race suffering. Also, with student activism now so prevalent, I think back to the days when my Black generation was in broken-down schools with broken down books and a group of broken-down passive voices. We didn't have the super communication of today, with cellphones or the Internet, and while I can't cite a poll or a study, my feelings are real, from having lived through those times and being the woman, I am today.

Each person is responsible for getting an education, becoming a self-sufficient adult, and pursuing the American Dream, whatever that dream may be in their life. While many African-Americans are progressing through education like never before, receiving better employment opportunities, and advancing economically in a more open and tolerant society, there are too many obstacles for poor rural and urban blacks to overcome. They are trapped in crime-ridden neighborhoods and low functioning schools. Achieving that stirring American Dream is almost unobtainable for too many, I am saddened about the crime and right-wing of society continuing to deny African American neighborhoods funding, leading to Black faltering and failure. I am so troubled by all of this.

We are all in this world together, my young friends, and I am right here with you.

Hattie

Equality is a must
For there to be
Trust
And
Individuality
And
Freedom
Hattie

Teen Empowerment Through Social Graces

My Dear Young Friends,

How are you feeling today? If you are working, was work okay? If you are attending school, was school, okay? Think about your day; could it have been better? You can do something to make every day better, and this is to be self-confident. So, you say you have all the confidence you need? I was young once and felt like that too. But, in reality, it was not the case. There are secrets every day that keep me going and boost my self-confidence, and I will let you in on them.

You see, my dear young people, confidence is the key to everything in life. If you feel self-assured, then you can overcome any obstacle, any difficulty that blocks your path. When you are confident in yourself, you can master any situation. You must have the mindset every day when you get up that you are ready to take on the world with kindness, respect, and brotherly and sisterly love. There is no anger in you. There is no jealousy in you. There is no envy and no hostility in your bones. You are happy with yourself, and you are not in any competition with anybody else. You are your person, and you have values, morals, and ethics. You are here to make the world better, and you have the confidence to do so.

When you make yourself better, you are adhering, living up to your standards and beliefs, and making the world better. You are nourishing the world with goodness and self-respect. You are helping the world breathe in social well-being. And do you know something, my dear young readers, you all are beautiful souls, and the world needs you. I need you. You see, when you are confident, your awareness is keen, and you are strong, mentally, and emotionally. It is the way the world works.

Another way to be self-confident is to carry yourself with grace and live your life as a nurturer of the world. Use your class and style, and confidence to become a person that is a joy to have around. It is empowering to be a humanitarian, care about others, and volunteer and help the young and the old and your friends and animals. Be useful to nature! Care about others as if they are you. It makes you confident when you care about others and make someone's life better. It is beautiful to be useful. It is beautiful and helpful.

I love how you are feeling right now, my dear young friends. You are feeling self-assured. It is one of the most beautiful feelings in the world. I don't know what time zone you are in right now. Perhaps you are in Africa or America or England or Mexico? Wherever you are, I feel your confidence, and I think your love for the world. If you are off to your day, have a beautiful day and, if you are about to go to sleep, sweet dreams to you.

And know, each day gets better with you in the world! We are all in life together.

Hattie

*I think about life
and learning
and I realize
those who are wise
cherish education
because they want
to be better
and succeed.*

Hattie

Hattie Isen

My Dear Young Friends,

How are you all today? I want to say something in this message to you. *"When the chips are down, you are not alone. I am here."*

Some of the most stressful events we can go through as a young person is losing a relationship, getting a low grade, or going through a traumatic event of losing a good friend. What you have to do when the chips are down is to be kind to all involved in the situation and be respectful. The real trick is to turn the loss into an opportunity for betterment and growth as a person.

Everyone goes through times when they feel differently. Sometimes, we scarcely have words to describe that feeling. We don't feel like ourselves. Perhaps we think in a state of panic and feel stressed out. We can feel like this when the chips are down. It is hard to make sense of what seems like unthinkable tragedies. Perhaps we are not supposed to understand such things. Maybe, we are just supposed to keep an eye on the realities of the horizon.

Remember, young people, you are not the ultimate life force. Your duration levels are human – no more and no less. Don't carry the world on your shoulders. Don't feel like you should already know something because you are a certain age. No age says you should know certain things at certain times in your life. Just know that ignorance doesn't protect you in life; education does. Knowledge is everything. School yourself in addition to your education. Learn as much as you can.

Enjoy school, work, and living. Bring joy to your family and friends. Award all with kindness and respect. Greet life with zest and enthusiasm. Keep a journal into the life you are living and see how you can improve your experience. Be grateful for what you have and study hard to get what you don't have yet. This part of my message reminds me of my daddy. My daddy was a hardworking man. His responsibilities were huge with a large family that he had to provide for in life with severe racial limitations. It was the fifties, and racial inequality was legal. Blacks were treated horribly. Good jobs for Blacks didn't exist. My daddy was serious-minded, and we, as his children, valued his attention and awarded him with the utmost respect.

I recall vividly the Christmas treats (usually fruit, candies, and simple toys) organized on chairs for each of us when we were children. That's all he could afford, but we took great joy and appreciation for what we got. Other fun times with daddy were attending the fall fair and family picnics. At the fair, daddy seemed to have taken pride in purchasing our treats, watching us enjoy rides, and keeping us together in a large crowd. I remember those days and the laughter we experienced. They were beautiful days despite the racism of the time. Life is bitter and sweet. You've got to try to enjoy life. We are all just visitors on this earth. Stay close to your family and friends and stay close to your faith. Life is sweet and bitter.

And remember, you can enjoy life sitting on a simple pile of hay and laughing with a good friend.

Hattie

*Life is what we make it.
Keep it simple.*
Hattie

*Talk to everyone in the same way,
no matter their skin color
or the faith they observe.
Treat everyone with respect
with everything you say —
every single word.*

Hattie

Hattie Isen

My Dear Young Friends,

I am troubled by today's world. Where is the respect for the old and young? Respect for life is missing today, and this saddens me very much. Back in my day, you never talked back to your parents or raised your voice at them or around them. You admired your parents and showed respect. But how do we show respect?

Kindness is a way of showing respect. Listening to someone without interrupting them is another way of showing respect. Being polite is still another way. Opening the door for someone is showing respect and showing up on time for a designated appointment. Respect for others leaves a beautiful impression on them. A person appreciates being respected. When you give someone respect, you are giving yourself a higher state of living.

My young friends, it would help if you respect yourself, too. If you don't respect yourself, you won't genuinely respect others, and you won't get respect from others. Self-respect is something we owe ourselves. It's the message that we send to the world, quietly asserting who we are and who we are trying to become, and how we'd like to be treated. You can't expect others to respect you if you don't respect your beliefs. This means you treat yourself the way you want to be regarded by the world. Remember, young friends, and it doesn't matter how old you are or how successful you've been at something in your young life, listen to the people around you. You still don't know it all, and neither do I.

You see, my young friends, I am always learning how to live. I definitely know being respectful to others, yourself, animals, and nature will make you a masterpiece. People will want to be around you. You will excel at school and in your career, and you will be highly successful. And you know what, you will succeed in a special kind of relationship of dating, and later marriage.

Remember, with your ideas and practices, respect is vital in your friendships and your relationships. Respect religions and cultures that are not your own. Respect local customs if you travel to another country. When we respect others, we are exhibiting style and charm, and social grace.

I want you to know, my young friends, that I respect every one of you.

Hattie

Party with kindness.
Party with love.
Party with respect.
And life
will be a party of joy.
Hattie

Teen Empowerment Through Social Graces

My Dear Young Friends,

Do you know what empowerment means? It is the process of becoming stronger and more confident, especially in controlling your life and claiming your rights. How does youth empowerment reduce barriers, close gaps – all gaps, promote loving relationships and social wellbeing, and eliminate racist attitudes and discrimination now and in the future? As you know, readers, there is an ethical and beautiful purpose of parenting and schooling that starts at an early age. Do you ever wonder why the current world is filled with hate, anger, despair, fear, trauma, threats, etc.? It is because of the lack of compassionate and caring leaders that have existed for far too long. Policymakers on the local, state, and national levels, corporations, and employers who continue to operate from old established racist policies aimed at keeping White folks at the top while oppressing people of color make society move in the wrong direction. Should we continue this trend?

Is there a need to address racism in a more thorough, intentional, and comfortable format instead of just having conversations? The racial injustice that has destroyed lives and oppressed so many existing "on a bridge over troubled waters" should be considered a serious one. I passionately believe that we owe more to you, my dear young friends. I strongly feel that we should protect your future – leaving it better than we found it. Let us advocate for giving you the love you deserve through guidance, education, and support.

Before we attempt to begin building loving, respectful, and trusting relationships, we need to focus on you. Who are you? What do you believe in? What are your strengths and talents? Do you have limitations? Where are you succeeding in life as a family member, a friend, club, team member, and a student? Do you think you have enough confidence to achieve most things in life, including tackling problems or social issues? What are your hobbies, and what do you enjoy doing leisurely? Are you a quiet and reserved person or an outgoing person? Think about your attributes, the gifts you have, your life talents. What are you good at in life? My sisters loved doing hair and were very successful at it.

Do you like art, and are you gifted at drawing? Are you talented at performing on stage? Can you sing? Can you dance? Are you good at math and science? Look at yourself with new optimism and excitement. You can change the world with your talents. Perhaps you love to cook and bring recipes to the world, and they will be comfort food and make people happier. The sky is the limit for you, my young friends.

"Self-education is the best education" is a quote my husband referenced occasionally. I, too, strongly suggest that you take advantage of extra time and engage in self-education. Initiate your ancestral family history. It all begins with you. Explore who you are and your real thoughts of what you believe and feel. Don't forget to strengthen any academia that need growth. Expand your research to your family's ancestral origin. Build an identity you are proud of and willing to share with the world.

My dear youth, your identity is incomplete without it! You may take after someone centuries ago!

Hattie

*I want to have friends
of all races
in all places
of all faiths.
Only then
can I say
I have lived
a full life.*
Hattie

Hattie Isen

My Dear Young Friends,

Where have all the flowers gone? Has love for each other, respect, and kindness become the stuff of illusion? But, is it also the magic potion of life?

Life and problems are shrouded in mystery as we wonder how did this or that happen. I am so sad that Black heritage has almost been lost to history. Why? Black people have had no comfortable place in society for such a long time. We have never had a place to hang our hats. We have just been a speck in the sea battling the waves of time. I fear we will never be able to have our full story told. My young friends do not tolerate limitations. Take education seriously. I did. It is important to learn! Strike it rich with fascination. You are bright. You are as smart as they come! Believe in yourself. I believe in you.

I want to say keep your fingers crossed in life, but unfortunately, luck doesn't happen for everyone. So, you have to make your good luck happen. You keep looking and keep dreaming, and you keep being productive. Do not become a string of risky choices. Be levelheaded. You are young, but youth goes by real fast. You must, in your young life, gain skill and experience. If a job or class comes your way and you don't like it, but it has benefits for you, do it for the sake of growth. Do it to get ahead in life. Also, always aim for betterment. Don't settle for staying with the first job, building debts, and feeling trapped. You can do better! Don't live in the survival mode. There have been many in life who have turned in their tuxedo or evening gown and turned to street begging so they could feel the ache of the poor. Only when you feel for others can we make this world better. Remember, there are those in life whose goals are simply survival.

Teen Empowerment Through Social Graces

There are times we feel empty. There are times we dodge gunshots. We are accused for no reason, but because of how we look and what we believe. It makes us scared and weary and devoid of life. Knowing that every day brings a new adventure and how you handle life is how life works. You must have a great attitude, be filled with kindness, and offer respect to yourself and others.

Dr. Martin Luther King walked respectfully in life. Filled with kindness, he warmly shook the hands of his enemies and friends. He had a dream – Honor Dr. King with yours.

And as for the flowers – where have all the flowers gone? If Dr. King were here, he would say keep looking for them. They are within your reach.

Hattie

*The truest pleasure in life
resides in making others happy.*
Hattie

Teen Empowerment Through Social Graces

My Dear Young Friends,

Are you kind? Do you know kindness makes people feel alive? Do you know what kindness is?

Kindness is a gleam of hope and a ray of sunshine. It is an embrace, a bouquet for no reason, a phone call to say hello, a kiss on the cheek. Kindness is a kind word of encouragement, a compliment, a smile, a note on the refrigerator that says to have a nice day. Kindness is rescuing an animal, comforting a child, listening to the elderly. My granddaughter, Sarelle, was asked to look at a dead ladybug on the bumper of their car. She admired it and turned her head to cough. My son asked, "Why did you turn away to cough, the bug is dead?" She stated, "but it's not nice to cough on it." On another occasion, a bird fell from a tree in their yard. It was unable to fly, and a few minutes later, it died. My granddaughter cried and wanted to bury it – appropriately to her. She is eight years old now. When she was five, and following Breaking News, she heard some unfavorable remarks about the news' character. Then she stated, "If I see Donna Trump, I am going to say I'll be your friend because he must be feeling sad."

My young friends, it takes a particular strength, a special person, to be a kind soul. A kind soul tries to see the good in things. A kind soul handles the madness in the world as a human being with respect. A kind soul does not fight off his opponents with slurs and anger. A kind soul talks it out without a raised voice. A kind soul does not bully or whip up violence or intimidation. A kind soul gently tells it like it is and is not afraid to stand by the truth. A kind soul is happy to offer what he or she can, as much as he or she can. A kind soul was my daddy. He went to a sock hop dance, saw my mother, walked across the dance floor, and offered her an apple! My daddy never went anywhere empty-handed. He was economically poor but kind-heartedly rich. He had a giving heart, a patient heart. He was simply a giving, kind soul.

My young friends, when terror floods the hearts and minds of those we know and those who are strangers, you need to reach out to them through the language of kindness. Kindness exerts a power that can change the air that we breathe. When you are kind-hearted, you are full of love, and love is such a beautiful thing. When we are full of love, we do not feel hate because hate is no match for love. Kindness and love go together. They are a strong pact. They are the forces that guide our thinking, feelings, and actions. When you are full of love and compassion and confidence and respect, nobody's racism can be stronger than your humanness.

Kind-hearted folks break down barriers and destroy hate. You are kind-hearted, my young friends. I can feel it. You are going to change the world with your presence and your heart and your kind soul. You are going to break down barriers. You are going to be kind and love everyone. This is not to say that you will not face challenges; they are always around, just waiting for your social graces and fruits of living. You, my dear young friends, will teach the world what it is like to be human. You are going to change the world.

My dear young friends, I must share with you a secret.

My greatest prayer is that I live to see this day.

Hattie

*There is an all-around
Season in life, and it is called
Kindness.*

Hattie

Can I lean on you
if I need support
if I feel weak
if I need to think?
Can I lean on you
and hold you
until the storm of racism
goes by?

Hattie

Teen Empowerment Through Social Graces

My Dear Young Friends,

What is racism? Racism is a lot of things. It is a master-race theory. It is a supremacist ideology. It is undisguised hatred. It ruins lives. It destroys the world, but more than anything, racism is a story of disappointment. It is a story of letting God down and our time in history down. Chiseled away by stereotypes, Blacks, people of color, Jews, and other minorities have had their dreams dashed or limited because of their faith or skin color.

Today, race relations in America are not what they were when I was growing up. We had broken down school books, back entrances and exits, tired old buses, and rusty unserviced water fountains. In my day, racism was vivid and legal. Today, it still exists but not like in my day. We all drink out of the same water fountain, go in and out of the same exits and entrances, but there is still racism. So, my young friends, what is the answer? What do we do?

Do we offer anti-discrimination training by providing support and strategies to trainers to hold classes to destroy racism? Can we change people who have racist agendas? Can we change the way a person feels? Can we change the way a person thinks? Ingrained racism causes behaviors that can be a catalyst for significant harm, disruption, and stress to anyone on the receiving line. But does it work?

Racism commands fanatical loyalty to a person or party and or both. Accompanied by hate and distrust and envy, greed, and oppression, it targets those retiring, those trying to build a decent job and home life, those just walking down the street to a mini mart. Heed the lessons of it, young people, because the United States has been the home of racial segregation for a significant part of its history.

Hattie Isen

I know you young people have had personal experiences of victimization, and its effects have had to hurt your health and well-being. Young people, I know you encounter racism and discrimination at school and on social media, and I am sad that racism remains an issue for you young people. How do you handle racism? How do you handle inequality? How do you take the ugly of it all? How do you address the injustice? These are excellent questions, and I am not sure that I still know the answers to these questions even today after I have lived a life of it. All I can say is that there is no way to justify racism.

Unfortunately, racism has become embedded in America's power structures, culture, education, and identity. It has been ingrained in the American fabric since the founding of this country. I have faced racism and discrimination all my life. I have woken up to it every day of my life. I am very familiar with the realities of racism, and I never let it stop me from succeeding in life.

Don't let it consume you. Don't let it frustrate you. Don't let it overwhelm you. And, don't let it stop you.

Hattie

*Don't blame others
for your mistakes.*
Hattie

Hattie Isen

My Dear Young Friends,

America is in a new direction, but we are not there yet.

Old fashioned stereotypes still exist today. Old social perceptions still exist today. You, my dear young friends, can make it all go away! Get to know who you are. Understand your ancestry. Be a person of color with pride or be of other ethnicities with pride. Understand your heritage—Cook foods of your culture.

There is a new awareness of minorities and the force we bring to America. People of color are a new force in America, and it is beyond the time that we are recognized. Black folks have suffered the cruelties of slavery and the chains of racism long enough. How long must we be reflected in slavery and with Jim Crow segregation? This definition reflects the long experience with slavery and later with Jim Crow segregation. We are tired of fighting for acceptance. It is our right to be part of the American bloodstream. We have a rich heritage of importance both to ourselves and to humankind on the whole.

Whites in the United States need some help envisioning the American black experience. They need to understand the Black American dream of equality. They have never lived it and cannot fully understand it. We need a national conversation on race and racial relations. But race is a sensitive subject. People get very emotional about it. But why?

Racists place a higher value on membership in a race than on individuality. Racists degrade those they loathe because of their religion or the color of their skin. Systemic racism causes widespread disadvantages in opportunity. Ultimately, throughout this country's history, American democracy's hallmarks – opportunity, freedom, and prosperity – have mainly been reserved for White people only. This is why there were Black entrances and exits. It makes me sick just thinking about this.

We cannot allow this to continue. The deep racial and ethnic inequities that exist today are a direct result of structural racism: the historical and contemporary policies, practices, and norms that create and maintain white supremacy. My African American culture, family, early development, and education were dominated by White Supremacy. There were many examples of how policies, decisions, and practices across the nation informed separatism and racial inequalities, especially in the south. Although court-ordered mandates were issued to protect people of color and grant them certain rights, White Supremacy, racial superiority, and inequality continued. It is still apparent today – listen to the rhetoric. Despite the inhuman treatment and efforts to deny equal access to quality education and lifestyle, I succeeded – and knowledge was the 'change vehicle' that got me there.

There is change on the horizon, my young friends.

Be that change.

Hattie

YOUNG PEOPLE,
We are all enslaved if one of us is enslaved.
Hattie

Teen Empowerment Through Social Graces

My Dear Young Friends,

We find ourselves encapsulated in the word freedom. We long to touch it, show our love for it, and feel it. We want to breathe it in deeply and exhale it for others. Freedom is beautiful, my young friends. How can we establish comfort zones and bring humankind to new levels of understanding in this world? How can we mingle our differences and throw them all into the kettle of respect?

Freedom defines us as human beings and is the most extraordinary collaboration against racism. We are all enslaved if one of us is enslaved. Every one of you must rally as one, break down barriers of hate and injustice and peacefully exercise your right to be free. But how do you do this? Armed with courage, confidence, respect, character, motivation, maturity, and social graces, you can conquer the racist monster. Remember, you are representing generations of children. Now, don't get me wrong, you can mess up and still have everything come out alright in the end, but you can't be reckless with your focus and desires.

You are human beings, my dear young friends. You must be caring, responsible, reliable, and live not for yourselves alone but for those who rely on you. Perhaps the family pet depends on you for its water and food and care, or a friend does from school for mentoring and academia or social support. Maybe an aging parent needs you to help with groceries or help walking the stairs. We have duties and obligations, but the responsibilities in life fill us with meaning and purpose. So, I ask you, my young friends, to master the art of maturity. Grow up with senses of worldliness and sensibility and allow your talents to flourish. Read and become educated. Education is the key to life. Education is the key to maturity. Master the art of

Hattie Isen

maturity, and you will always be respected.

You are filled with good temperament and talents. You have a business mind but a loving heart. You want the good things in life, but you won't steal them; you will earn them. You will work hard for them as my daddy did. You are strong in mind like my mommy was. And you are filled with loving hearts as our ancestors were. They were slaves and worked hard and handled the burden of their circumstances. They lived another day so you could be free.

The vulture of racism will bow its head to you when it sees you are better than it. You are filled with inner beauty, generosity, and goodness. You are kind. You feel compassion, and you are learning that you are right about a lot of things. But you also know you are wrong about a lot of things. You are sure of yourself but have a desire to learn from others. You will bring a loaf of bread to those starving because you believe in doing the human being thing.

I am proud of all of you.

Hattie

*If there was no bigotry,
if there was no hatred,
if there was no evil,
we could feel love
and show off our hearts.*

Hattie

What does it mean to put yourself in another person's shoes?
How empathic are you?
How can you show empathy toward others?

Hattie

Teen Empowerment Through Social Graces

My Dear Young Friends,

What is empathy? Empathy is the ability to feel your feelings. It is the ability to be sensitive to others. My young friends, it is the ability to understand what someone else is feeling. It allows you to go through another's person's pain and agony and suffering and feeling it as if you have gone through it all. Empathy is an essential element of compassion. When you are compassionate with yourself, you feel better. When you are human with others, they feel better, and you feel better. Understanding is an active process that relieves suffering, both for yourself and others.

Young friends, when someone is yelling at you in your face, use compassion. Compassion is a skill. You demonstrate that you heard them and show understanding by saying, for example, "You seem upset, and it's okay to express it. Do you wish to share your feelings in a softer voice, I will show you the same respect. I am here for you." You ask the person confronting you what you can do to help them with their life and how you can support them emotionally. When we practice empathy, we practice respect. When we practice care, we practice understanding.

Both empathy and compassion are skills. Our brains are not wired to reflect and feel each other's emotions. We must work at it. We read evident and subtle clues from others, and we continuously broadcast our emotional states for all to see. We read others, and they read us – body language through facial expressions, tone of voice, posture, scents, and texts. We use our emotional states to attract and repel people, and we are appalled by and attracted to others based on the emotions they project. We read signals from people and form opinions by first impressions.

Hattie Isen

Young friends, can we save the world by being empathic? One of our under-appreciated natural powers is the ability to feel what another person is feeling and collectively what another nation is feeling. If we see somebody being happy, we feel their happiness. If we see somebody suffering, we feel their suffering. We have this ability.

Saving the world generally begins with keeping your world. You can build your powers of empathy and compassion by paying attention to your feelings. When you feel yourself suffering from sadness or stress, notice your emotions, and use them to generate sympathy for others. Understanding your feelings increases your ability to understand others. Feeling compassion for yourself increases your ability to draw on that when it is time to help others. I was there to help my siblings, and they were there to help me. When my younger brother drove, I let him borrow my car to take his test.

When you are not consumed with your feelings, you can use your empathic powers to focus on others. Notice how they look, listen to what they say, and imagine what they are feeling. Put yourself in their place. Noticing and guessing what another person is feeling and adding a little compassion when they seem to suffer can go a long way toward making things better for both of you and the world.

My young friends, please don't be selfish. Selfishness is a thief. It robs you of your soul. When you are selfish and self-centered, you are walking down the wrong road in life. You feel that superiority is your road, your path. Being selfish is not the way to deal with situations. Be a giving person. The world does not revolve around you. Selfish people are not successful people. Selfish people are lonely people.

Teen Empowerment Through Social Graces

We do much of this attracting and repelling, reading, and broadcasting, subconsciously. If somebody is screaming in our face, we can reasonably interpret that they are angry. They feel anger, broadcast anger, read anger, and understand that they are mad. We do that so quickly and so regularly that we don't think about it. What we tend to think about is what that person is screaming about. Empathy happens behind the scenes, but we can quickly bring it to our attention, which creates an opening for compassion.

If somebody is screaming in our face, we may have difficulty noticing our empathy and remembering to use compassion. We naturally become defensive to protect ourselves from the potential and actual violence of the anger. We would likely feel the anger so strongly that we would get angry ourselves. We could respond with any emotion, depending on who we are and who is yelling at us.

What feelings we feel and project in response to the anger will affect the initial outrage. If we remember to use compassion, we can find a suitable answer to make the situation better. When we practice compassion, we find ourselves caring about our emotional states and others' emotional states. We recognize how much we and those around us suffer, and we acquire techniques that help us engage with and relieve the suffering.

Remember young people to practice compassion; we begin by noticing suffering. If we are suffering, we practice kindness toward ourselves. We look into our nightmares to see what may be causing them. We imagine what would alleviate the suffering. We think about what we can do to help ease the suffering. If there is something we can do, we do it. If we notice suffering in another person, we do the same thing for them. Like any skill, the more we practice compassion, the better we get at it. Remember, young friends; understanding comes from the heart. When we practice empathy, we notice suffering. We notice suffering by feeling it. When we practice compassion, we ease suffering. We won't always know what we need to do to ease another person's or our suffering, but with practice, we get better, and as we practice, we suffer less, and so do our friends.

Remember, empathy is feeling with someone; sympathy is fishing for them. Just because we dislike what someone does, does not mean they don't have a story worth sharing. How many TV shows out right now are about putting yourself in real situations? Empathy fuels our curiosity and reveals a more nuanced way of looking at the world. To approach problems empathetically is to keep an open mind. It is as simple as that. We don't just watch television shows; we feel what the characters are experiencing. We feel like we are part of the show.

Empathy teaches us not to give up on one another to embrace our flaws. It expands our ideas of who we are and who we're capable of becoming. We don't need it to be explained; we need to experience it and thank God for it.

Strive to be compassionate. Remember happy times and celebrate accomplishments. Celebrate good friends and good people. Live to be empathic and dare to be human. I know you can do it. Leave a rose on the doorstep of a sick friend.

Compassion is a beautiful thing.

Hattie

*Joy comes to those who learn
to appreciate what they have
and have the motivation
to work to get what they want.*

Hattie

Hattie Isen

My Dear Young Friends,

So, you will have jobs in your life that you may not like. You will have classes at school that you may not like. How do you handle it all? You show the world what you are made of, and that is love and hope and motivation. You can control it all because you are confident, filled with self-respect, and respect for others, and you are loaded with kindness. Nothing can keep you down. You are highly motivated, and you want to succeed in life, and you will succeed in life. The following are my suggestions.

Go to work with not a good attitude but a great attitude. Do not be filled with negativity. Whether you want to be there or not, having a positive attitude is what it is all about. If you go to class or work gloomy, you will have a bad day and make the course or job even worse. On the flip side, showing up to work smiling and happy will also spread through the office, and before you realize it, it might not be such a wrong place after all, and you might even start liking the class or job.

Life comes with likes and dislikes. Choose to find a balance – but leaning on the side of preferences. Look forward to something in your day to balance what you don't like. When my siblings and I were picking cotton, it was hard work. We didn't like it, but we looked forward to mommy bringing treats for us to eat like sweet yams, and it made working so hard not so bad. And we knew that that collective work by all of us would bring joy to our parents. Life was easier for all of us. Remember, it is up to you to keep going in life with an attitude you can be proud of and show off to others. Remember to show your best side in life, and people will admire you for it. Also, take a moment to recognize the other aspects you love about your experience and remember that our jobs and classes are only a small slice of the pie.

Remember, my young friends, we are only tourists here on this earth. Nothing is permanent in this life. So, your lousy class or job is not for eternity. Everything in life is a steppingstone. Keep pushing yourself. You must know that this is the only way you will get somewhere. Remember, education is the vehicle that drives you to success! The stops you make en route are the grade level steps, kindergarten through college, and beyond.

Take life seriously. If you don't like your life, reinvent it. Become known for tackling severe problems and having the right mindset. My young friends know that life is fundamentally crazy. You might think of it as a jungle of developmental issues across our life span – puzzles to be solved. That's why your social graces are needed. Develop a sense of humor for coping with things and know laughter is the best medicine.

Hattie

How do we fight for equality?
How do we live with things that are unfair?
How do we handle lies
And deceit year after year?

How do we handle the choices
That are made supposedly on our behalf?
How do we learn to love
When important topics we are not even asked?

How do we function in society
When people look at us with scorn in their eyes?
How do we handle racism
And a world that is not always wise?

How do we handle life moments
That make us not at our best?
How do we handle life
When life puts us to the test?

Hattie

RESPECT

Respect is also called esteem.
And it is a beautiful thing.
It is a positive feeling that conveys
A sense of admiration
Or valuable qualities
That somebody has
Regardless of the color of their skin,
Their place of worship,
Or their age.

Respect is something that you give someone
Or it is something that you give yourself.
And care cannot be compared
To anything else,
It is where dreams start.

*For if you have respect for someone or
For yourself,
It is like nothing else.
You feel love so clearly.
You see.*

*So, my young friends,
I give you respect.
In this book,
Lots of respect
From you
To me.*

Hattie

No gangs
No bullying
and
No violence.
Hattie

Teen Empowerment Through Social Graces

My Dear Young Friends,

What do you want in life? You want to be educated. You want to be wise. You want to be successful. You want to be liked, and you want a peaceful life. But how do we get all these things? We accomplish these things, to begin with, by establishing a positive and supportive school and work environment. Trending data over the past few decades suggests that bullying has made the school environment fearful and hostile. Bullying can be a big issue for schools since it creates a poor school environment for students to learn and negatively impacts teaching. If teachers cannot teach in a positive environment, your understanding is limited, and education is the key.

The bully mentality is not you, my young friends. You have more focused goals and achievement aspirations and no time for bullying. However, let us not forget that each of us could one day lose hope due to life's adverse circumstances and become a bully. I pray that it does not happen to you. Bullying is evil and stems from those who are not respected, not confident, insecure, ignorant (do not know), and do not care about other people, although they did not plan to be this way. Many bullies have been traumatized and are simply victims of circumstances. But this is not you.

You have clear goals in life. You are someone who can be trusted. You are loved. (Bullies are loved too but are not on the receiving end due to the disconnect with supportive relationships at the time. I believe in human potential with a little tender love and care.) You are different as you do not harm others to get what you want. You employ acts of kindness to express respect and bond with others so, your wants are achieved through your humane social graces.

Sometimes, youth who have been bullied and abused emotionally and physically may have also suffered shame and rejection and discrimination and have internalized humiliation. This is what they know and have experienced. Sometimes it is turned into anger and violent behavior. This results from the lack of a caring and supportive community, including appropriate counseling. Some of these youth have given up on life, mostly if parents or guardians lacked relevant parenting skills and/or gave up on them.

Frequently young people accept and turn to gangs for love and security, putting them at risk of making counterproductive choices to a safe and happy future. Sometimes, in their vulnerable state, they are easy targets to be victimized by other adults. I learned from counseling with similar youth in the past that many reluctantly participate in gang-related activities to be popular, thinking it would be temporary but find themselves trapped. Once inside, they are attracted to the opportunity to make money through drug trading and selling. They have lost their individuality. They feel there are no other options. Because of their lifestyle, they lose friends and lack exposure to positive peer influences. They lose the beliefs they once had in themselves. They find themselves caught up in violence and hatred. It is the gang culture. Please understand that not all bullies become gang members.

The hardcore bullies and the violent street gangbangers think they're powerful and full of wisdom, but this is not the wisdom for you as understanding does not work this way. Insecure people want to be heard also; they want power, want to be heard in the worst way and valued, and want to be the one that everybody goes to for advice. But they go about it the wrong way, and they end up in prison or dead because what they wanted was vengeance. And the legacy of despair and violence continues to infect the next generation because they cannot break the cycle of hopelessness and insecurity. This, too, is a culture that needs to be understood, supported, and cared for. Is this culture the result of systemic racism? Do all youth have access to a socially just society? More specifically, do they and their families have adequate food, sleep, wages, education, safety, opportunity, institutional support, health care, childcare, and loving relationships to maintain a lifestyle without starving or feeling economically trapped, devalued, disrespected, and discriminated against? It would be good to know the real answers relative to those who bully.

    I just know that bullying is not you.

Hattie

*When you treat someone wrong,
It shows that you are
Upset with yourself.*
Hattie

RESPECT IS IN THE LISTENING.

*I thought that I would try it.
I didn't know how I'd do.
I thought that I would try it.
It would be something new.*

*I walked into the room,
and a discussion was at hand,
and I stood there just watching,
I thought, let me listen
the best I can.*

*So, I sat there listening,
And being mindful of all being said.
And I did the best that I could,
To process the discussion in my head.*

*So, I listened
And that was what I did to learn.
And the more that I listened,
The more I heard.*

*And then I waited
Until someone was done talking before I'd respond.
And I realized all of my interrupting,
Was so wrong.*

I realized that my listening,
Was the key to the new me.
I felt so enlightened.
It was a feeling too good to be.

I was in the here and now.
Distractions don't stand a chance.
I am so open-minded.
My words are in a dance!

I no longer judge prematurely,
I am filled with lessons.
I sense the topics so much better,
And ask all the right questions.

Because I am a listener,
And the listening is now me.
I am mindful and respectful,
To be a good listener makes me free.

To learn better
And respect to all I share,
I am a different person,
Now that I kindly lend an ear.

Hattie

Teen Empowerment Through Social Graces

My Dear Young Friends,

I want to talk about a few more things before closing. The first thing I want to talk about is acceptable behavior. Good behavior exists so that we don't hurt people with our words and actions. We don't interrupt someone who is speaking, we don't call them derogatory names, we don't make fun of them, and we don't physically harm someone. It is essential that we interact positively with others and greet others with kindness, despite their race and faith.

I believe in good manners. I believe in the offering of food to friends and family before you help yourself. I think in considering others' feelings and being the person that others like, admire, and respect. The best thing in life is to make a good impression on all those you know. Be helpful and be hopeful for someone. Be attentive to their needs and let them share their feelings with you. Be a confidant. Be someone who gives sound advice. And more than anything, fill the world with love and care and kindness to all. Give heart to the elderly, animals, nature, and yourself.

Always be on time when keeping an appointment, showing up for school, and with your classes. Be dependable. Make sure you come through for people. Be full of interesting conversation. Educate yourself in and out of school. Speak intelligently. When you speak intelligently and show up on time, you will be respected. Participate in life with enthusiasm. You have a right to your own opinion but listen to the views of others.

Learning about the outside world is not easy. We all face daunting challenges. Take each challenge one by one and stay true to yourself. Life is what you make of it. Keep true to your values, ideals, and goals in life. Handle rejection gracefully. Cheer others on, and most importantly, know that I am rooting for you to be a success!

Life is about keeping promises. It is about being honest, kind, and courteous, and respectful. It is about supporting your friends with positive feedback. Life is about your integrity and about the respect you have for yourself. Life is about apologizing and saying thank you. It is here I want to say something else about thank you. Thanking others is one of the keys to having good manners. Send thank-you notes or emails whenever someone does something nice for you, or telephone to express your gratitude. This simple act will help build lasting relationships with family and friendships with friends. When someone compliments you, the best response is a simple "thank you." And don't forget "Please," "Excuse me," and "You're welcome," which are other marks of good manners. Life is about learning to welcome people with disabilities and being helpful.

Are you a giving person? A fundamental rule of good manners is to give. Think about what you can give to others and remember that the most precious gifts cost nothing. Kindness costs nothing but will make a dog wag its tail and a person smile. When you meet someone, you can always think of a genuine compliment to give. A "Hello" or "How are you?" is not enough. You can also share your undivided attention and interest with others. You can be generous with words of warm greetings, sympathy, and lots and lots of love.

Remember that a small person boasts about their accomplishments. There is no need to have an ego in life. Don't live life as a billboard. You don't need to self-advertise; let your respectful behavior and your deeds speak for themselves. Listening to others and not interrupting shows who you are as a person. What you say can hurt you as well as hurt others. Don't embarrass yourself or others with your words. Think before you speak. Add every day to your life and the life of others. Be a calming influence on your family and friends, and your pets. Master self-control and have empathy for others. Always act your best with courtesy and politeness, and respect.

I was young once. Racism and poverty were in my way. But I was going to be somebody someday. I met the challenge. I prayed to God, loved my family, and felt empowerment from the sun and clouds in the sky. I imagined a world of beauty and love. I imagined myself in this world. I studied. I studied hard. I wanted to live in a world that celebrated who I was. I found this world, and you will, too. And, I am with you every step of the way.

Remember, there is a light in all of us to be shared and treasured. Life is all about social graces. When you have good manners, you make your presence sparkle. Make your way in the world. But more importantly, make your mark with your heart in the world. And, I am with you every step of the way, believe it.

Hattie

*Young friends, there is a role between etiquette
and communication.
Part of etiquette and manners is communication.*

Hattie

Teen Empowerment Through Social Graces

My Dear Young Friends,
I have enjoyed this path of you and me.
And remember how I believe in you.
Thank you all for reading,

Hattie

*Give with
All your heart
And
Live with all
Your heart.*

Hattie

EPILOGUE

My Dear Young Friends,

Those large numbers of enslaved Blacks were held captive as slave labor and forced to produce crops to create wealth for White America; it saddens me to this day. It remains an American truth. Even centuries on, we are still touched by slavery and the remnants of it all. The legacy of slavery is a big ugly blemish in America's history. The slave side of the story is your story, my young friends. But Blacks have not been the only enslaved people throughout history. The Jews were enslaved, and only in the 1930s were enslaved labor products in the death camps. Centuries of slavery, followed by decades of institutional repression, has haunted both cultures. Racism is haunting, but let's talk about plantation life.

In some of my previous writing pages, I mentioned the impact of slavery, not just to those who labored and built this country to benefit White America, those who were mistreated, devalued, and denied education, beaten, and murdered, separated from families, etc. Later, generations feel the pain, humiliation, and scars they suffered as descendants of slaves. My excellent, great grandparents shared it all through the years. Of course, it was a quiet oral history. Those kept in bandages were discouraged from sharing mistreatments. They worked long hours and had to adhere to the slave owners' standards.

Slaves complied to avoid being sent to another owner far away from family or other cruel punishment. The word obedient was frequently mentioned by older ancestors to imply that slaves had to be submissive to the masters, slave owners. The ingrained racist attitudes were used toward my father, other relatives, and the educational practices that I observed and experienced. With a level of forgiveness, my anger and humiliation toward the forces against my ancestors transformed toward a compassionate and kindhearted will for the betterment of all.

Either we choose to keep the anger and bitterness inside or let go by replacing them with self-confidence, kindness, and respect that each of us is capable of. You see, my friends, these are the smarter strategies that will result in mental, physical, and social well-being for all of us. Embracing all individuals, those you agree and disagree with, those you face with conflicts, those who use racial slurs toward you, and those who enslaved your ancestors, you have the power to help them find favor with you. It is the most humane way to help build a beloved community, now and for the future. So, practice the fruits of life, the fruits of the spirits, and lead the way in making life beautiful. Remember, life does not have room for racism.

We must realize that racism still exists, and what can we do about it? Can we be a nation, a collective nation, a unified nation, if we are a racist nation? Can we have a fully functioning economy, a functioning education system if we are still a nation of repression? Can schools perform in racist neighborhoods? It would help, my young friends, if you did not allow any more racist blows to hit this nation. You must keep communication lines open with those you agree with and those you don't agree with. You are responsible for moving this nation forward. You join us in moving this country forward and establishing its image as a vital and robust society of equality and presidential healthcare, and presidential education for all.

Care about your rights and your roles as young people. Be gems of society. Polish your social graces, light up the banner of respect in life, let kindness be your path, and let love be your future. My young friends, only when love is your future can you truly be the change that Dr. Martin Luther King died for, my young friends. Enact commonsense reforms, create loving communities, and change the system through nonviolence. Make Dr. King proud.

Hattie

www.ingramcontent.com/pod-product-compliance
Lightning Source LLC
Chambersburg PA
CBHW070100100426
42743CB00012B/2611